OSCAR PETERSON TRIO

CANADIANA SUITE

CONTENTS

Cover courtesy of LIMELIGHT Records.

Transcribed from the original recording by Jack Jordan

ISBN 978-0-634-09985-4

HAL•LEONARD®
CORPORATION
7777 W. BLUEMOUND RD. P.O. BOX 13819 MILWAUKEE, WI 53213

In Australia Contact:
Hal Leonard Australia Pty. Ltd.
4 Lentara Court
Cheltenham, Victoria, 3192 Australia
Email: ausadmin@halleonard.com

Visit Hal Leonard Online at
www.halleonard.com

CANADIANA SUITE

BALLAD TO THE EAST

No. 1

By OSCAR PETERSON

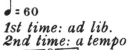

No. 2

LAURENTIDE WALTZ

By OSCAR PETERSON

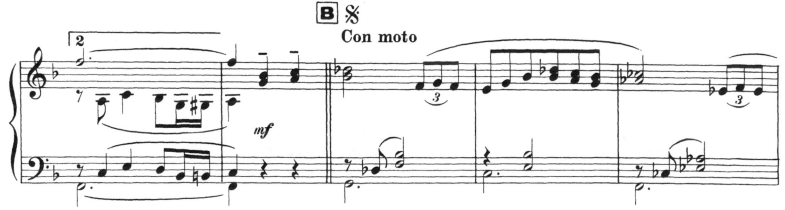

6

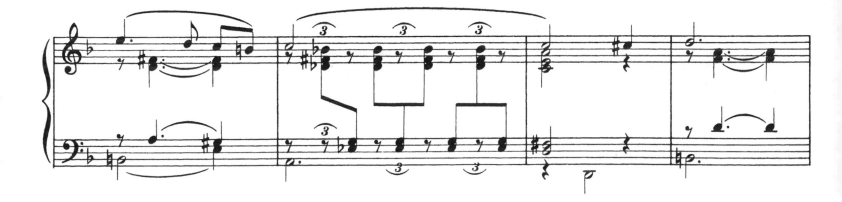

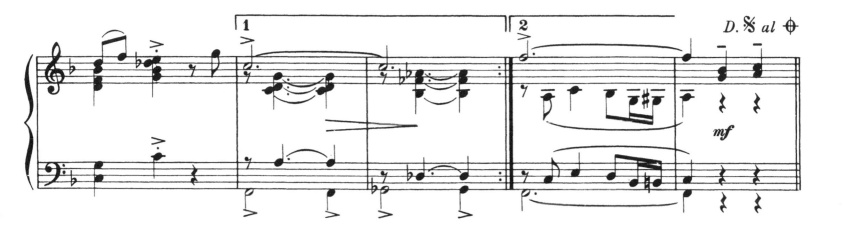

No. 3

PLACE St. HENRI

By OSCAR PETERSON

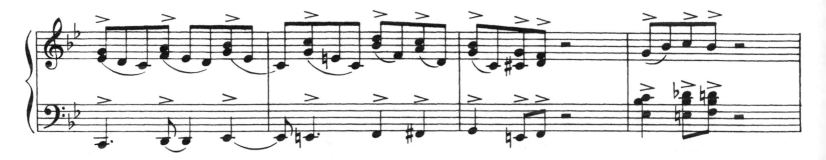

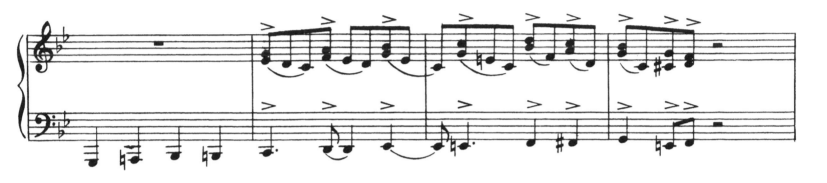

No. 4

HOGTOWN BLUES

By OSCAR PETERSON

The passage from **A** to **B** gives the harmonic skeleton of the whole movement

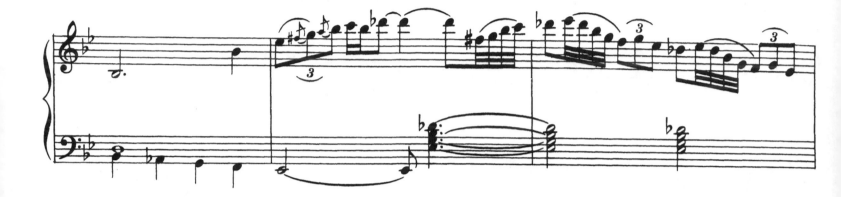

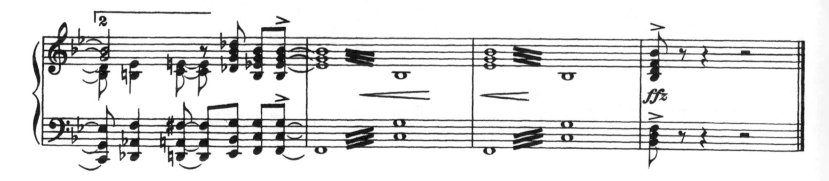

No.5

BLUES OF THE PRAIRIES

By OSCAR PETERSON

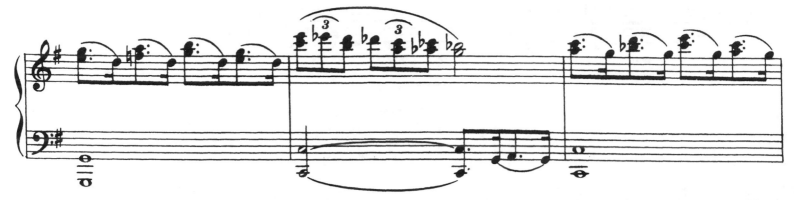

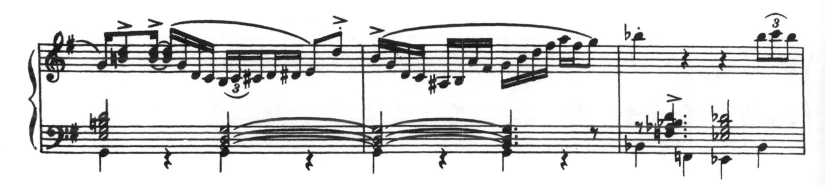

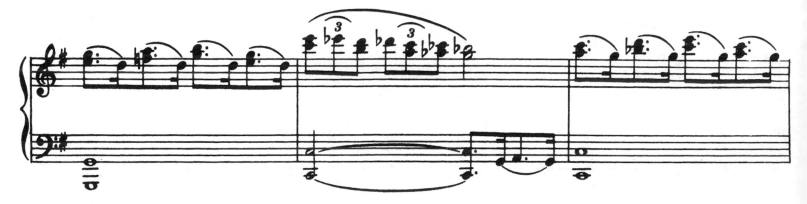

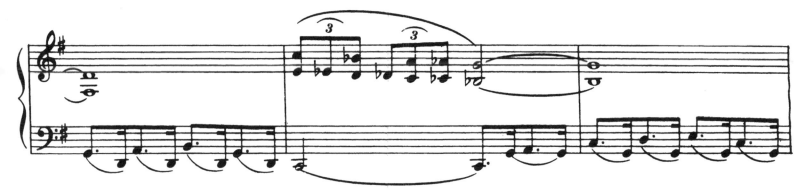

No. 6

WHEATLAND

By OSCAR PETERSON

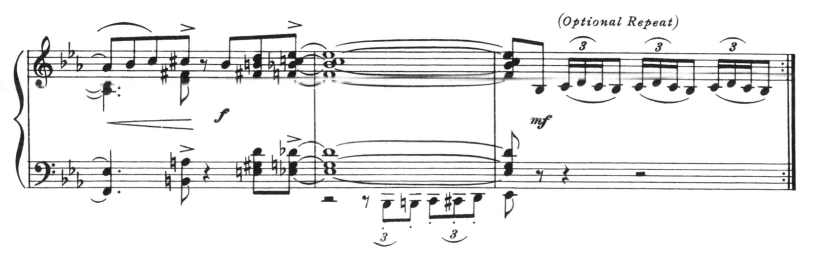

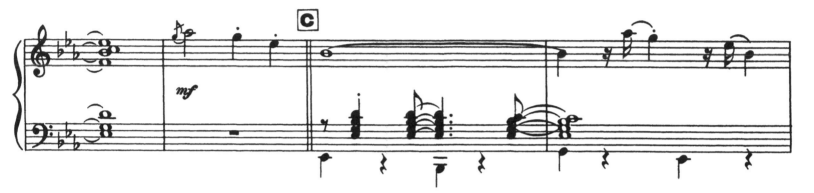

Note that bass line from C to D is intended as a harmonic guide, not to be played.

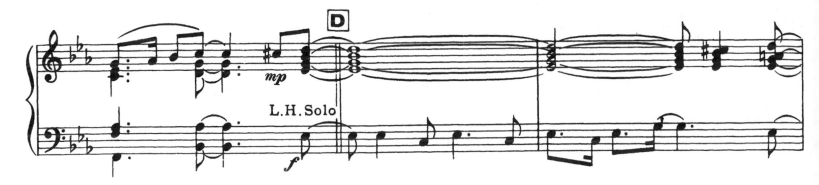

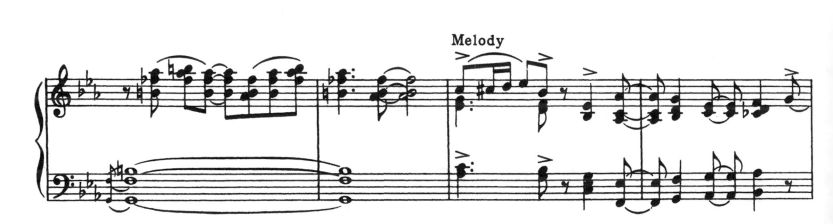

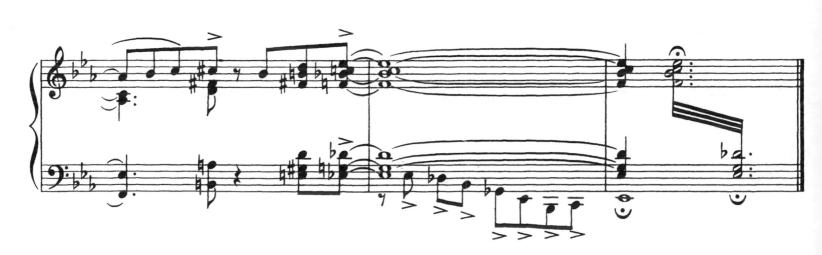

No. 7

MARCH PAST

By OSCAR PETERSON

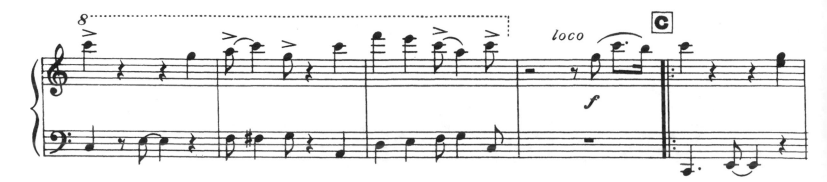

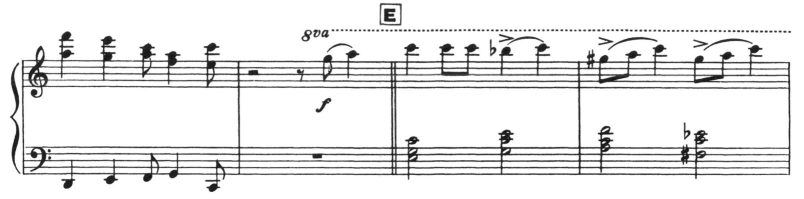

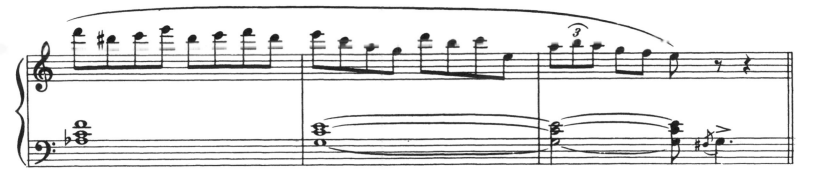

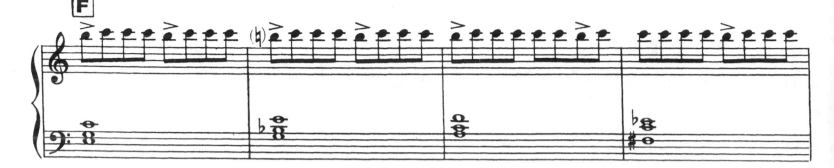

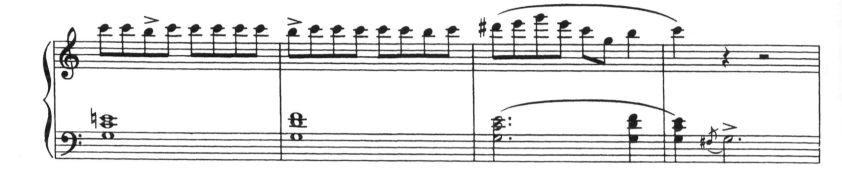

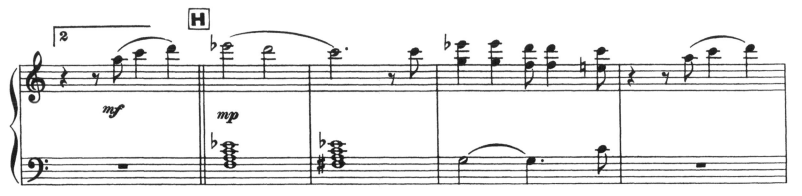

No. 8   # LAND OF THE MISTY GIANTS

By OSCAR PETERSON

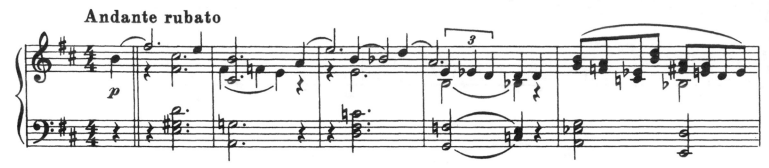

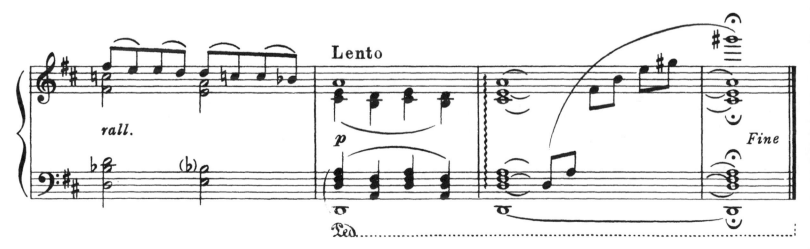